MEXICO FOR KIDS
PEOPLE, PLACES AND CULTURES
Children Explore The World Books

SPEEDY
PUBLISHING

Speedy Publishing LLC
40 E. Main St. #1156
Newark, DE 19711
www.speedypublishing.com

Copyright 2015

The official name of
for Mexico is the United
Mexican States.

Mexico is a federal republic in North America. Mexico is the fifth largest country in the Americas.

The Mexican people have varied origins and an identity that has evolved with the succession of conquests among Amerindian groups and later by Europeans.

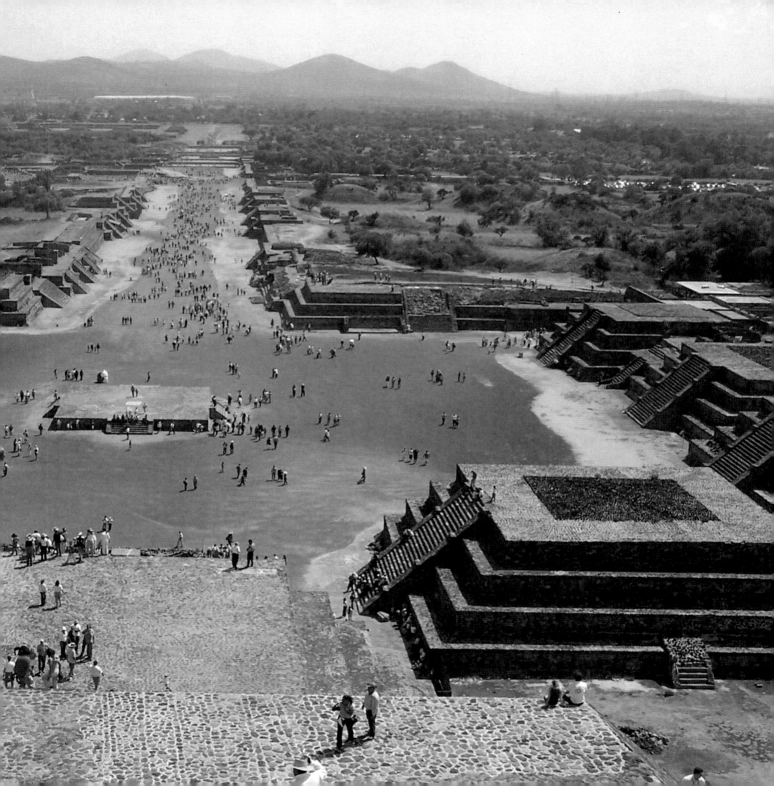

The Basilica of Our Lady of Guadalupe is a Roman Catholic church visited by several million people every year, especially around 12 December, Our Lady of Guadalupe's Feast day.

Chichen Itza is one of the most visited archaeological sites in Mexico. Chichen Itza was one of the largest Maya cities and it was likely to have been one of the mythical great cities.

Pre-Columbian Mexico was home to many advanced Mesoamerican civilizations.

The earliest human artifacts in Mexico are chips of stone tools found near campfire remains in the Valley of Mexico and radiocarbon-dated to circa 10,000 years ago.

Chichen Itza was a large pre-Columbian city built by the Maya people. Chichen Itza is located in the eastern portion of Yucatán state in Mexico.

Dominating Zócalo square, the massive Mexico City Metropolitan Cathedral is one of the oldest and largest churches in the western hemisphere.

For thousands of years, Mexico's Indians such as Aztecs and Mayan were the only people who lived in Mexico.

A torero is
a bullfighter
and the main
performer in
the sport of
bullfighting as
practiced in
Mexico and
other countries.

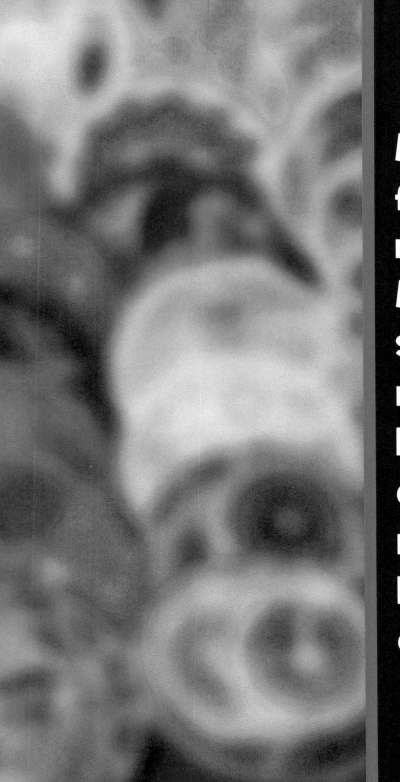

Mariachi is a form of folk music from Mexico. Most songs are about machismo, love, betrayal, death, politics, revolutionary heroes and even animals.

The size of a Mariachi group varies depending on the availability of musicians.

It is common for people in Mexico to make and sell items in open markets.

Weaving and embroidery are among the traditional crafts of Mexico's native Indian people.

Women bring brightly decorated clothes into the towns to sell in the markets.

Day of the Dead is a Mexican holiday celebrated throughout Mexico. A common symbol of the holiday is the skull.

ans eat a
y of spicy
that are
flavored
nilies.
meals
rved
rtillas.

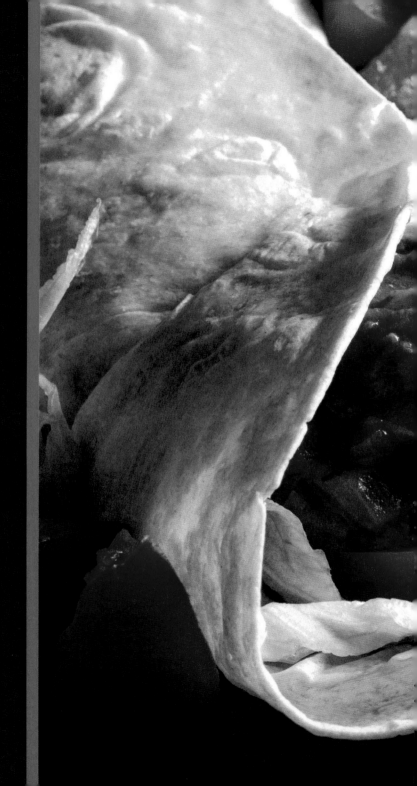

Mexico is the 11th most populated country in the world with around 117 million people.

Made in the USA
Coppell, TX
29 January 2021

49115036R00026